W9-DDK-070

Aunt Sally's Tried and True Home Remedies

Aunt Sally's Tried and True Home Remedies

Gramercy Books

New York • Avenel, New Jersey

Copyright © 1993 by Outlet Book Company, Inc.
All rights reserved.

This 1993 edition is published by Gramercy Books,
distributed by Outlet Book Company, Inc.,
a Random House Company,
40 Engelhard Avenue, Avenel, New Jersey 07001.

Random House
New York • Toronto • London • Sydney • Auckland

Designed by Bill Akunevicz Jr.

Printed and bound in the United States of America

Library of Congress Cataloging-in-Publication Data
Aunt Sally's tried and true home remedies.
p. cm.
ISBN 0-517-09114-3
1. Herbs—Therapeutic use. 2. Herbal cosmetics.
I. Gramercy Books (Firm)
RM666.H33T75 1993 92-39269
615'.321—dc20 CIP

8 7 6 5 4 3 2 1

Contents

Introduction

Among Aunt Sally's most treasured posses-
sions was her special notebook of home remedies. Friends and relatives always knew they
could go to her for the best advice on simple
and natural ways to relieve life's common ailments. Fortunately for us, members of Aunt
Sally's family have preserved her notebook
and have permitted us to publish it in this
edition so that her invaluable and highly effective remedies are available to everyone
who needs them.

According to Aunt Sally, colds, congestion,
headaches, and indigestion may all be helped
by teas made from such herbs and spices as
ginger, thyme, allspice, peppermint, and rosemary. The book begins, therefore, with in-
structions for making comforting herbal teas.
Aunt Sally's other hints suggest remedies for
sunburn, hiccups, tired eyes, and foot problems. To promote soft and healthy skin, Aunt
Sally explains how to utilize buttermilk, diluted lemon juice, cucumber, honey, and
even oatmeal.

It is not recommended that Aunt Sally's suggestions should take the place of modern medical advice from a physician, but the tried and true remedies in this modest volume are based on old-fashioned wisdom and the use of natural, readily available ingredients.

THE EDITORS

Avenel, New Jersey
1993

Herbal Teas

No matter what the ailment or physical dis-
comfort, Aunt Sally believed a hot, comforting tea, made with herbs, spices, or flowers, is
often the best remedy. Such teas are easy to
make. Simply crush the appropriate dried
herb or dried flowers, or use powdered spices.
Put a heaping tablespoon of the substance
into a tea ball. Let it steep in a cup of hot
water for about 15 minutes. Whole, dried, or
fresh herbs may be steeped in hot water, but
the tea should be strained before drinking.

Aunt Sally had a list of therapeutic teas and
their uses. You may find it helpful as a quick
reference in matching the restorative powers

of various herbs, spices, and flowers to common ailments.

Tea Made from:	Good for:
Allspice	Nausea
Aniseed, crushed	Coughs
	Congestion
Basil, dried	Nausea
Camomile flowers	Isomnia
	Indigestion
Caraway seeds	Congestion
Cloves	Nausea
Dill	Upset stomach
Ginger, powdered	Indigestion
Mint, fresh	Headaches
Orange blossom buds	Insomnia
Parsley, fresh	Indigestion
	Congestion
	Coughs
Peppermint, dried	Indigestion
	Flatulence
Rosemary, dried	Headaches
Spearmint, dried	Flatulence
Thyme, powdered	Scratchy throat

Calming a Cough

Nothing is more annoying than a cough, particularly at night. Here are some of Aunt Sally's favorite cough remedies. If a cough persists for more than a week be sure to consult your doctor.

Just before going to bed, dissolve 1 tablespoon of black currant jelly in 1 cup of hot water. Drink immediately.

This homemade syrup often helps to control coughing. To make the syrup, put 1 large lemon in a saucepan. Add hot water to cover.

Bring to a boil, then reduce the heat and simmer for 15 minutes. Remove the lemon. When it is cool enough to handle, cut it in half and squeeze the juice into a glass jar. Stir in 2 tablespoons of glycerin and 1 cup of honey. Take 1 teaspoon of the syrup as needed. Be sure to stir thoroughly before using and keep the jar covered.

A tea made with licorice root will often soothe a sore throat and relieve a cough. Try drinking a cup of the tea every 6 hours.

An effective, old-fashioned remedy for soothing a sore throat is to gargle with hot water in which salt has been added. Dissolve 1 teaspoon of salt in a cup of hot water.

This is a cough remedy that Aunt Sally often recommended. Peel a large turnip and cut it into slices ¼ inch thick. Spread honey on each slice. Put all the slices into a bowl. Set aside for 3 hours. Every 4 hours take 1 tablespoon of the syrup that collects at the bottom of the bowl. (Be sure to keep the bowl covered.

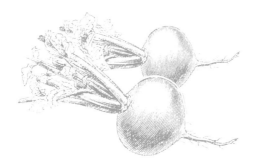

For a tickling cough, mix 2 teaspoons of apple cider vinegar in a glass of water. Take 1 tablespoon every 4 hours.

A mixture of 1 teaspoon of grated horseradish combined with 2 tablespoons of honey will soothe a cough and make a good expectorant.

Onion juice mixed with honey also relieves a cough and acts as an expectorant.

A tea made from crushed aniseed makes a good decongestant. It helps to loosen mucous and calm a cough.

Caraway seeds brewed into a tea is an effective expectorant.

Coping with a Cold

There's still no cure for the common cold, but there are some simple remedies that can make you more comfortable and, in some cases, may even reduce the period of suffering.

Cold symptoms can often be relieved by drinking a tea made from ginger and honey. To make the tea, steep 1 tablespoon of coarsely grated, peeled ginger in 1 cup of boiling water. After 15 minutes, strain the tea and add 1 tablespoon of honey.

To relieve cold symptoms, add a heaping tablespoon each of dried sage and camomile and $1/2$ tablespoon of thyme to a quart of boiling water. Then inhale the vapors of the steaming blend.

Aunt Sally always insisted that chicken soup can alleviate cold symptoms. Today this folk remedy has been proven to help unclog nasal passages. So when the first symptoms of a cold appear, make a big pot of chicken soup and have a cup of the hot soup several times a day.

Rose water mixed with a syrup made from mulberries is excellent for a sore throat.

A cold in its early stages may sometimes be warded off by drinking a glass of cold water in which $1/2$ teaspoon of baking soda has been dissolved. Repeat 3 times at hourly intervals.

Today we know that vitamin C can help reduce coughing, sneezing, and other cold symptoms. Aunt Sally recommended drinking lots of orange, grapefruit, and cranberry juice, which are in fact rich sources of vitamin C.

A sore, irritated throat can be relieved by gargling with salt water every 4 hours. Dissolve 1 teaspoon of salt mixed into a glass of very warm water.

To soothe a sore throat, try a tea made from dried thyme. Thyme is also useful as an expectorant.

Treating Digestive Distress

Aunt Sally made copious notes on the relief of common problems of digestive distress. All of her simple and natural methods are highly effective in combating minor bouts of nausea, indigestion, and flatulence.

Peppermint tea is an all-purpose digestive aid, good for gas, heartburn, and nausea. Make the tea with crushed dried peppermint leaves.

Eating watercress promotes a good appetite and it helps to cleanse the digestive system.

A tea made with powdered ginger will aid digestion.

Camomile tea is a good digestive aid, especially if taken after a heavy meal.

To relieve indigestion, sip cold milk very slowly.

To avoid heartburn, during a meal drink $^{1}/_{2}$ glass of water to which 1 teaspoon of apple cider vinegar has been added.

Celery juice is good for the digestion and can relieve gas and indigestion.

A tea made from dill may help calm an upset stomach.

Chew on a few sprigs of raw parsley to help settle an upset stomach.

A tea made with powdered allspice can relieve nausea.

Clove tea is also helpful in relieving nausea.

Eating an apple or two each day will help prevent diarrhea.

A cup of tea made from dried basil can relieve gas and nausea.

Drink warm water to which a few drops of cinnamon oil have been added to relieve diarrhea.

Easing a Headache

Aunt Sally claimed that a headache can be relieved by placing a poultice of apple or potato slices on the forehead for 30 minutes. To make the poultice, wrap the fruit or vegetable slices in a piece of cheesecloth. Wet the cloth and place it on the forehead. Cover with a warm cloth.

A tea made from fresh mint or lavender will often relieve a mild headache.

Rosemary is an excellent headache remedy. Brew the dried herb into a tea or apply the essential oil directly on the temples.

Treating Minor Bruises, Muscle Pains, and Inflammations

Aunt Sally always had a bottle of witch hazel on hand, and for good reason. Witch hazel helps to reduce inflammations. It soothes minor cuts and bruises. It makes an excellent astringent. And it generally helps to promote healing. It has also been known to reduce the prominence of veins.

A tea made from slippery elm bark is a natural pain reliever.

Apply eucalyptus oil or fennel oil to aching joints to reduce the pain and swelling caused by rheumatism or arthritis.

The oil from the garden variety of thyme—and in fact the entire plant—has beneficial antiseptic and disinfectant qualities.

To relax stiff and sore muscles, try rubbing into the affected areas a mixture of $1/2$ cup of olive oil and $1/2$ teaspoon of rosemary oil.

Comfrey helps promote the healing of sprains and strained muscles. A prepared extract or ointment of comfrey is a superb traditional treatment for insect bites, minor abrasions, and other skin irritations.

Encouraging Sleep

Almost everyone experiences the occasional night when it seems impossible to fall asleep. Often a cup of herbal tea made with camomile, peppermint, lemon verbena, or red clover helps to induce sleep. But there are other old-fashioned remedies you might try.

Aunt Sally insisted that nothing induces sleep better than honey. For chronic insomnia she recommended 1 tablespoon of honey every evening after dinner.

Another old-fashioned remedy is apple cider vinegar and honey. In a jar, combine 4 teaspoons of the vinegar and 1 cup of honey. About 30 minutes before bedtime take 2 teaspoons of the mixture.

Camomile tea has a calming effect and acts as a sedative.

A tea made with dried orange buds makes many insomniacs sleepy.

Hot onion soup will often induce sleep. Have a cup at bedtime.

To prevent sleeplessness, take a warm bath just before retiring. Or walk for 30 minutes in the open air.

To induce sleep, try wetting a cloth with cold water and laying it on the back of the neck.

Another method of promoting sleep is to drink a cup of hot milk or a glass of cold buttermilk before retiring.

To avoid insomnia, try eating a light snack an hour or so before bedtime. Avoid sugar, but a piece of fruit, some bread, and, of course, a cup of warm milk can be helpful.

Stopping Hiccups

Everyone hiccups every so often. Even doctors are not really sure what causes hiccuping, but everyone agrees that an attack is pretty annoying. Hiccups will usually stop in a little while without treatment, but there are many home remedies. Here are some you might try.

Suck on crushed ice.

Try holding your breath for 20 seconds.

Pull hard on your tongue.

Chew and swallow dry bread crusts.

Try tickling the roof of your mouth with a cotton swab.

Gargle vigorously with cold water.

Aunt Sally always insisted that a teaspoon of sugar works like magic to stop hiccups.

Dealing with Foot Problems

According to Aunt Sally, corns and bunions may be softened and relieved by making a salve from equal proportions of lard and baking soda and applying this at night before retiring.

A good remedy for corns is an ivy leaf steeped in vinegar and bound over the corn. Cover with a slightly oily cloth and tie securely around the toe.

Pineapple juice applied topically can help dissolve a corn.

The juice of radishes is effective in reducing painful corns. Apply it for several days.

To help aching feet, soak them in 1 gallon of hot water to which a few cups of very strong peppermint tea has been added.

To soften calluses, soak your feet in diluted camomile tea; then wash them with soap and water.

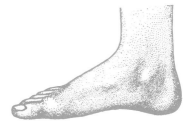

Alleviating Eyestrain

Sitting in front of a computer monitor or a television screen for many hours can strain your eyes just as much or more than quilting or embroidering or other needlework did in Aunt Sally's day. She had some remedies for refreshing tired, strained eyes that are well worth trying. To get the full benefit of these remedies, lie down with your feet raised.

Aunt Sally always insisted that eye pads soaked in rosemary tea are most effective. To make these, steep $1/2$ teaspoon of dried rosemary in $1/2$ cup of boiling water for 10 minutes. Dip two cotton pads in the tea. Place a pad on each eye for 15 minutes.

To reduce puffiness around the eyes use cotton pads that have been moistened with cold, strong camomile tea.

Eyestrain may be helped most by avoiding the problems that cause it. Use a soft, not dim or glaring, light to read. Take your eyes off your work at least once every 30 minutes. Rest your eyes by closing them for a few minutes every so often. Blinking your eyes frequently cleanses them.

Relieving Mosquito Bites

A mosquito bite can be very annoying. Here are some simple remedies that usually reduce the swelling and relieve the itch.

Moisten 1 teaspoon of salt with enough water to make a paste. Apply the paste to the bite.

Apple cider vinegar, witch hazel, raw honey, or lemon juice will relieve the itching and swelling of an insect bite.

An ice pack will also help to control the swelling and itch of a mosquito bite.

Dissolve 1 teaspoon of baking soda in 1 cup of cool water. Wet a clean cloth with the solution and place on the bite for 15 minutes.

Soothing a Sunburn

In the days before sunscreens, when people didn't know how dangerous too much sun can be, sunburns were common, particularly in the first days of summer. Even today some people do get careless. If you're one of them, here are some old-fashioned remedies that you might find helpful.

Cover sunburned arms or legs with plain baking soda, petroleum jelly, or olive oil and bind with a cloth or gauze.

Use cucumber juice or apply sliced cucumbers to relieve sunburn.

A paste of cornstarch and water applied to the sunburned areas can be soothing.

Thin slices of cucumber or raw potato feel cool and can help to reduce inflammation on small sunburned areas.

Aunt Sally swore by lettuce water to soothe sunburned skin. Boil about 12 lettuce leaves for about 10 minutes in a saucepan of water. Strain the liquid into a bowl. Chill in the refrigerator for at least 2 hours. Dip a cotton pad into the liquid and then gently stroke the irritated skin with the wet pad.

Plain yogurt is cooling as well as soothing. Apply it to all sunburned areas. Leave it on for about 15 minutes, then rinse it off in a cool shower. Gently pat the skin dry.

Hand Care

In Aunt Sally's day, as well as in ours, clean-
ing, gardening, and working around the
house could result in irritated, rough, grimy,
or dry hands.

Aunt Sally suggested wetting dirt-encrusted
hands and rubbing them with soft brown
sugar. After doing this, rinse the hands in
soapy water and dry them thoroughly.

If fingernails have become stained or discolored, soak them in a pint of warm water to which 1 teaspoon of lemon juice has been added.

To strengthen brittle nails, dip them in warm olive oil for a few minutes each day.

To soften hands, keep a dish of oatmeal near the soap dish in the bathroom. Rub the oatmeal freely on the hands after washing. This will soften the skin. Or use cornmeal in the same manner.

Another method for softening the skin is to rub your hands at night with honey, then slip on a pair of large gloves.

Lemon juice or the juice of ripe tomatoes will remove most stains from the hands.

If your hands are always moist from perspiration, bathe them in a weak solution of vinegar or lemon juice, which will act as an astringent.

Honey may be used on the hands when the skin is dry, hard, and rough. Moisten the hands and rub the honey in well. After 10 minutes wash the hands thoroughly with soap and water.

Rub chapped hands with linseed oil.

For dry and chapped hands, mix a little sugar with baby oil and rub the concoction into the hands for a few minutes. Then wash with soap and warm water.

Skin Care

The softness and freshness of skin was a con-
cern for Aunt Sally and many members of
her household. Over the years she noted a
number of methods to maintain a healthy
complexion.

Almond oil helps to soften dry skin, according
to Aunt Sally.

Add camomile flowers to the bath to improve
the skin tone.

Witch hazel brightens and tones up the skin; but it should not be used on dry or sensitive skin.

Use cucumber juice to whiten and soften the skin.

The garden variety of thyme may be used in bath water to aid skin tone.

A tea made with watercress and allowed to cool helps to reduce skin blemishes.

Buttermilk is useful for fading freckles. It also relieves itching and local skin irritations.

A bath in hot water, in which 2 cups of baking soda have been dissolved, gives the skin a velvety texture.

Strawberry juice is effective in whitening the skin. It also removes tartar from the teeth.

Making Facial Masks

Even in Aunt Sally's day, women knew that a facial mask can do wonders for the complexion. And if, while the mask is doing its work, you lie down with your feet up and your eyes closed, it will also help relieve tension. Here are three masks easily made at home. After you remove the mask apply a moisturizer.

An apple-honey mask is great for a combination skin. Peel and core a large apple then puree it in a blender or, if you prefer the old-fashioned method, grate it finely into a bowl. Mix in 3 tablespoons of honey and 1 teaspoon of dried sage. Blend well, then apply to your face. After 15 minutes rinse the mask off with warm water.

An avocado mask is easy to make and is particularly beneficial for dry skin. Simply mash a peeled and pitted avocado. Smooth it onto your face and neck. Leave the mask on for about 15 minutes, then remove it with warm water.

If your skin is oily use a yeast mask once a week. To make the mask, dissolve enough dried yeast in warm water to make a thick paste. Apply to the face and leave it on for about 20 minutes. Remove with warm water.

Hair Care

Women used hair conditioners, beautifying rinses, and natural color enhancers before any of the newfangled commercial products were available. Try some of these.

For oily hair, use a rinse made from 1 quart of distilled or rainwater to which the juice of 2 lemons has been added.

Mayonnaise is an excellent conditioner for dry hair. Before shampooing, massage $^1/_2$ cup of mayonnaise into the hair. In the old days a towel was then wrapped around the head, but it's much easier today to just cover the hair with a plastic bag. After 20 minutes un-cover the hair, rinse with warm water, then shampoo thoroughly.

Perhaps the best of all hair shampoos is made by beating the yolk of an egg into 2 cups of warm rainwater. Apply at once, then rinse off with warm water.

To add shine to blonde hair, mix 4 table-spoons of lemon juice in 2 cups of cool water. Use as a rinse after shampooing.

For brunettes, strong, cold tea is a wonderful rinse. Use after shampooing.

Beer, even if it's flat, is a wonderful setting lotion. Put the beer into a spray or pump bot-tle. Spray it on shampooed, towel-dried hair, then blow-dry or style in the usual way. Your hair will be nice and shiny, and the odor of beer will disappear as soon as your hair dries.

A cucumber conditioner guarantees healthy-looking hair. Puree a cucumber. Massage the cucumber into shampooed, towel-dried hair. Leave for 10 minutes, then rinse thoroughly.

To prevent split ends, use yogurt. After shampooing, massage $1/2$ cup of plain yogurt into the hair. Comb the yogurt through, then rinse well.

Even in Aunt Sally's day, there were a number of ways to enhance the color of one's hair.

Brunettes can darken their hair color and cover gray by using a sage rinse. To make the rinse steep 4 tablespoons of dried sage in 2 cups of very hot water for 3 hours, then strain. Pour the rinse over clean, dry hair about 12 times. Let hair dry, then rinse with warm water and dry hair in the usual way. Apply the rinse once a week until the hair has reached the desired color. To maintain the color use the rinse once a month.

A camomile rinse will add highlights to blonde hair. To make the rinse, steep 4 tablespoons of dried camomile in 2 cups of very hot water for 2 hours, then strain. Pour the rinse over clean, dry hair about 12 times. Leave the last rinse in the hair for about 20 minutes before rinsing with warm water. Dry in the usual way or in the sun.

Aunt Sally's Old-Fashioned Hints for Healthy Eating

"Meat once a day is sufficient during the hot weather—especially for children."

"Onions are a wholesome and nourishing vegetable, and when properly stewed are not indigestible."

"Oatmeal porridge and milk, bread and milk, crushed wheat, rice, barley meal, peas, and cornmeal are all wholesome and nutritious foods and, with a little fruit or tomatoes in season or lettuce and an occasional soft-boiled egg, should constitute the chief food of children."

"Heavy cakes, sweets, and pastry are to be avoided, or eaten sparingly or on special occasions."

"A small quantity of fluid should be taken with meals, but a cup of tea or coffee or a tumbler of water after a meal is good."

"People require a greater amount of animal and solid food in cold than in hot weather. In the heat of summer, eat less meat and more vegetables and fruit. In extreme cold, fat should be more freely used. As a rule, one meal of animal food daily is sufficient. The other two meals should consist of vegetables, rice, oatmeal, rolled wheat, hominy, seasonal fruit, milk, and so on. Peas, onions, and beans are especially rich in nutritive matter. Sugar, in moderation, to sweeten dishes, is not objectionable. Wheat flour is much to be preferred over 'extra-fine' flour."

"Ground fruits and vegetables, such as strawberries, lettuce, and tomatoes, should always be washed before being eaten uncooked."

"As a rule people do not drink sufficient water. When perspiring freely, a larger quantity is needed than at other times."

"The diet of someone actively engaged in open-air activity should be more plentiful and generous than that of the sedentary office worker. But there are many examples of health and strength maintained by the use of the simplest food only. In times not far gone by, the farm laborers of Scotland—a stalwart and hardy people—lived almost entirely on oatmeal and milk, while the agile and wiry Spanish mountaineer thrived on black bread and onions."

"Tea and coffee are much alike in their action upon the system, and when used in excess give rise to many unpleasant nervous symptoms, headache, and indigestion. When of good quality, freshly prepared, and used in moderation, they are most refreshing and gentle stimulants, relieve fatigue, and sustain the system under unusual mental or physical strain."

"Pure water is the most suitable beverage for common use. A tumbler of hot or cold water taken upon rising in the morning, before food, is invaluable. It cleanses the stomach and prepares it for the exercise of its function. A moderate quantity may be taken with meals; in excess, especially if iced, it retards the digestion. Between meals it may be used freely—the quantity depending upon the nature of the diet and the amount of exercise and perspiration. It would be an advantage to drink water more freely than is generally done."